RESEARCH
AIRPLANES

RESEARCH AIRPLANES

Testing the Boundaries of Flight

Don Berliner

Lerner Publications Company • Minneapolis

Page 1: A Douglas D-558-II Skyrocket being launched from a B-29 carrier plane (see pages 30-31)
Page 2: A Bell X-22 V/STOL airplane with its ducts pointed forward for level flight (see pages 48-50)

Library of Congress Cataloging-in-Publication Data

Berliner, Don.
  Research airplanes.

  Includes index.
  Summary: Describes how airplanes, designed for research
and testing, are used to explore new areas of flight.
    1. Research aircraft—Juvenile literature.
  2. Aeronautics—Research—Juvenile literature.
  [1. Research aircraft. 2. Airplanes] I. Title.
  TL567.R47B47   1988   629.1'2'072   87-17238
  ISBN 0-8225-1582-2 (lib. bdg.)

Manufactured in the United States of America

1 2 3 4 5 6 7 8 9 10 97 96 95 94 93 92 91 90 89 88

System 5/89

Contents

A Grumman X-29 (see pages 40-41) is carefully checked by aeronautical engineers and technicians.

1

The Research Airplane

Some airplanes are not meant to carry passengers or freight. They are not war planes or personal planes or sport planes. There is no thought of putting them into mass production and building many more like them. They are research airplanes.

Research airplanes are meant to help people learn how to build better airplanes. They are built to explore new areas in the science of flight and to solve problems that are expected to arise 5 or 10 or even 25 years from now. For this reason, researchers must have a clear vision of the future and know enough about trends that are expected to develop so they can visualize airplanes that might be flying when their young children are adults. Some research planes are used to learn how to design airplanes that will fly faster than any other airplane

has ever flown. Others are designed for learning how to develop airplanes that can take off from a space as small as a parking lot instead of a long runway.

Designing a Research Airplane

To learn how airplanes might be able to fly faster or more efficiently, scientists and aeronautical engineers research current airplane designs. Once they have pinpointed a problem with an existing design, they must decide how to go about solving it. First, they try to find out if an entirely new type of airplane is needed. Or, perhaps an airplane flying today can be *modified*, or changed. For example, engineers may decide to remove a plane's original wings, engines, or

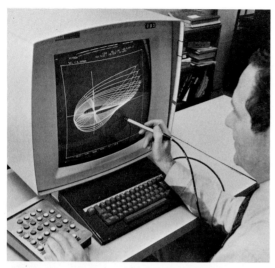

Computers such as the ones shown here are used to design research airplanes.

control surfaces and replace them with new, untried ones.

Engineers design new planes using computers as electronic drafting tables. A design for a new airplane is programmed into the computer, and then changes are made on the screen with a special hand-held device. Computers allow engineers to find out how a new or modified airplane will fly even before it is built, which saves both time and money.

When the engineers have developed a good design, a large scale radio-controlled model of the real airplane may be built. A model can be redesigned easily and quickly, and no

In a wind tunnel, pieces of string are glued to a model to show the direction of the air flowing over an airplane. If the strings fall straight back, the air is flowing correctly.

one will be injured if it crashes. Models of several different designs are often tested at the same time in order to find out which one works best.

If a design is substantially new or different, it may be necessary to build a *flying test bed* before trying to fly the actual research airplane. A flying test bed is a construction of the main parts of the new airplane that will be tested to see if the new design ideas will work. Attached to strong cables to keep it from going too high, a test bed may fly just a few feet above the ground.

If all the preliminary steps have proven the basic idea to be sound, a research airplane is built. It will be carefully constructed by hand by the most experienced technicians available, and many changes will be made during its construction as the engineers continue to adapt and improve its design. At the beginning, no one knows exactly what the finished plane will be like.

Above: Technicians prepare a small model of a research airplane for tests in a wind tunnel. Held by the technician on the left, the radio control box will change the model's *attitude*, or angle with the ground, during the test. Below: Designers work with a larger model with forward-swept wings.

Preparing for the First Flight

Flying a research airplane is a job for a highly trained test pilot—a pilot who will be able to feel every little movement of the plane and sense immediately if something is about to go wrong. Because the purpose of the airplane is to try out new design ideas, the pilot will be exploring an unknown aircraft a little bit at a time. In order to learn as much as possible about the airplane, it will carry in-flight recorders and telemetering equipment to radio data to technicians on the ground who will monitor everything that happens in the air.

Everyone involved in the first flight of a research airplane is under great tension. Years of hard work and millions of dollars are at stake. The airplane is checked from nose to tail and checked again. A single loose wire, a missing connector, or a tiny flaw in the computer software could bring a quick end to the first flight—and the entire project.

The Test Flights

If the first flight goes exactly as planned, it will be surprisingly dull! There will be no spectacular climb to amazing altitudes, no blazing passes just a few feet above the runway, and no sensational aerobatic display. Far too much has gone into the project to risk losing

a plane during a few seconds of reckless flying.

The pilot will begin the flight by carefully accelerating to takeoff speed and then gradually climbing to a safe altitude for some cautious maneuvers to see how the new plane handles. The modern test pilot is more of an engineer than a cowboy and will be

Colonel Albert Boyd buckles on his parachute before flying 624 mph (998 km/h) in a Lockheed P-80R to set a new world air speed record in 1949.

concerned with checking the many dials on the instrument panel and reading their numbers every minute or two. Even if the purpose of the airplane is to fly faster than any other plane has flown, it will not be flown at its top speed during the first few flights. Only after the airplane has been flown slowly for takeoff and landing will it be safe to fly faster.

After the first test flight, the mechanics and engineers will check the entire outside of the plane and then open the access doors to get to the inside. Anything that was broken during the flight will be fixed or replaced, and any part that did not work properly will be redesigned. For this reason, a second test flight may not take place for several days or weeks.

Once the plane's low-speed handling characteristics have been proven safe, the test pilot will start to push the throttle forward, a fraction of an inch at a time, as much as the test program permits. In the 1930s, it was not uncommon for a test pilot to take up a new design, point its nose straight down, and, with its engine wide open, fly as fast as possible. Numerous airplanes shed their wings in such wild tests, and many good pilots died.

While the experimental airplane is undergoing tests in the air, an identical airplane will undergo different tests on the ground. In a large laboratory room, the *static test vehicle* will be mounted on special equipment that will bend and twist every part thousands of times to simulate the stress of takeoff, climbing, descending, and landing. To see how they stand up to the forces of actual flight, the test vehicle's wings will be covered with hundreds of bags of shot or sand several times heavier than the total weight of the airplane. In order to discover its breaking point, this nonflying airplane may be tested until it is destroyed. These tests will reveal what parts of the test plane might fail if it were maneuvered too tightly.

By the time the airplane is ready to fly again, so much will be known about it that there should be very few surprises. But since the research flights may take the plane to unknown speeds, altitudes, or maneuvers, there is always the chance that something totally unexpected will happen. In such instances, the people on the ground will be glad that an expert test pilot is in control.

The lifetime of most research airplanes is fairly short. They either work well and complete their tests, or they fail and are grounded while another plane is prepared for testing. When an airplane has finished its work, it may be modified for another project or broken up so engineers can use its parts in other airplanes. If the plane is successful and helps to advance our knowledge of flight, it may be presented to an aviation museum so people can see it up close and better understand what it did and how.

Orville Wright lies in the *Flyer* and Wilbur Wright runs alongside to steady the wing in the only photograph of the first successful motor-powered flight.

The First Research Airplane

The first piloted airplane that flew—the Wright brothers' 1903 *Flyer*—was also the first research airplane. Orville and Wilbur Wright were inventors more than they were pilots. They had built and flown gliders for several years, and they probably knew more about flying machines than anyone else in the world at that time.

When the Wright brothers built their 1903 *Flyer*, they equipped it with instruments to record how fast the plane flew and how well its engine worked. If it flew, they wanted to know why it flew. After their successful flight on December 17 at Kitty Hawk, North Carolina, the Wright brothers knew even more about what made an airplane fly properly. They had learned about airplane engines and about propellors. They had discovered how to make an airplane fly where they wanted it to go and how to keep it from crashing into the ground.

The Wright brothers were the first airplane builders who tested an airplane like real scientists, and the planes they built and flew were true research airplanes. When they had learned all they could from their first plane, they retired it and built a better one.

This photograph of the Grumman X-29 research airplane was taken just after its completion and before its successful first flight on December 14, 1984.

2

High-Speed Research Airplanes

Ever since the first airplanes lifted off the ground nearly 90 years ago, men and women have worked hard to make them fly faster. At first, designers increased speeds by making planes more streamlined so the air could flow around them more easily. Then they had to use bigger engines.

The first airplanes, however, were anything but streamlined, and they had all of their parts—engine, wheels, even the pilot—sticking out. Soon it became obvious that putting the plane's components inside the plane where they would not disturb the flow of the wind would make the plane go faster. The original bundles of sticks and wires that connected the wings to the tail were covered to make a *fuselage*, or body. The early pilots were convinced they needed to feel the wind in their faces in order to fly well,

so they sat in cockpits with their heads poking out in the wind. In the 1920s, airplanes with clear canopies over the pilot's head finally became popular.

In order to operate without overheating, an engine must have air flowing over it. Airflow causes wind resistance, however, so metal *cowlings* were built around the engines to make them more streamlined. *Baffles* directed cooling air around the engine parts, and the center of the propellor was covered by a piece of metal called a *spinner*.

The next important development to be tested on research airplanes was retractable landing gear. Although an airplane's wheels are needed for takeoff and landing, they can be pulled up into the wings or fuselage during flight so as not to create any wind resistance. Today, all but the slowest of airplanes have retractable landing gear.

As airplanes traveled faster, their rough, uneven covering was made smoother and more uniform. This, too, cut down on wind resistance. Sheet aluminum replaced fabric, which distorted easily, and the rivets that held the aluminum in place were made *flush*, or even, with the covering so they would not interfere with the airflow.

Faster airplanes also needed bigger engines. The 1903 Wright *Flyer* had only a 12-horsepower (9-kilowatt) engine, but, by the late 1930s, some airplanes had 1,000-hp (745-kw) engines. And engines of 2,000 hp (1,500 kw) were becoming common by the mid-1940s. The introduction of the jet engine brought about even greater advances in power levels. A jet engine's power is measured in pounds of thrust instead of horsepower, and the first jet engine used on airliners produced over 50,000 pounds of thrust (222 kiloNewtons), which at top speed equalled about 100,000 hp (75,000 kw).

It was the mysterious *sound barrier*, an imaginary wall airplanes were thought to encounter when they flew at the speed of sound—750 miles per hour (1,200 kilometers per hour) at sea level and 650 mph (1,040 km/h) at high altitudes—that forced designers and engineers to build pure research airplanes. They wanted to know exactly what would happen when an airplane flew that fast.

Some experts thought it might be impossible to control an airplane when it reached *Mach 1*, which is how scientists refer to the speed of sound. Others thought the air would pile up in front of the airplane to prevent it from going any faster. But everyone agreed that only a carefully designed and powerful airplane would stand a chance of breaking through that unknown barrier.

Subsonic Airplanes

At first, all airplanes flew at *subsonic* speeds, or slower than the speed of sound. When airplanes neared Mach 1, they started to fly strangely. Some would go into a dive from which it was very hard to recover, and others acted like their controls were working in reverse. Engineers wanted to design and build airplanes that could fly at the speed of sound, and their efforts resulted in the first high-speed research airplanes.

deHavilland deH.108 Swallow

British engineers who wanted to build a faster jet airliner decided to build a plane with swept-back wings and a vertical tail—but no horizontal tail. To test their idea, they built three small single-engined jet Swallows.

The deH.108 used the fuselage and engine of a deHavilland Vampire jet fighter with special wings and tail. This small, streamlined airplane, the most modern-looking plane at that time, first flew in the spring of 1946.

Then trouble struck the second Swallow. On a flight to attempt the world air speed record, the plane crashed and was destroyed. Pilot Geoffrey deHavilland, Jr., the son of the company's founder, died in the crash.

Engineers wanted to find out why the Swallow crashed so they could make sure the plane's problems were corrected. Tests in a huge wind tunnel showed that an airplane of this shape wanted to tuck its nose under while flying close to the speed of sound. If the plane had been flying at high altitudes, there might have been a chance to slow it down and get it back under control. But Geoffrey deHavilland had been skimming over water when he ran into trouble, so he had no chance to recover from the dive.

By 1950, the two other Swallows had also crashed on test flights. But thanks to some very brave test pilots, engineers now understood what the problems were. When jet airliners with swept-back wings began carrying passengers, they were safe. But because of what engineers had learned from testing the Swallow, these passenger jets all had horizontal tails.

This early research airplane—the deHavilland Swallow—later crashed on a high-speed flight, killing pilot Geoffrey deHavilland, Jr.

Major Marion Carl stands alongside the Douglas D-558-I Skystreak in which he has just set a world air speed record.

Douglas D-558-I Skystreak In the United States, scientists and engineers were also exploring the mysteries that lay near the sound barrier. The first U.S. subsonic research airplane to fly was the Douglas Skystreak, a U.S. Navy airplane with straight rather than swept-back wings. The Skystreak first flew early in 1947, nearly one year after the Swallow. After it had been in the air less than 10 hours, the navy decided it worked well enough to attempt the world air speed record.

In August 1947, Navy Commander Turner Caldwell flew the Skystreak at 641 mph (1,026 km/h), which was faster than any official speed record. Then a few days later, Marine Corps Major Marion Carl broke that record in the same airplane with a series of runs timed at 651 mph (1,042 km/h). Suddenly, the Skystreak was famous.

The three Skystreak models made dozens of flights to provide information that made it possible to build faster and safer airplanes. One crashed during testing, but the other two were retired and put on display—one at the U.S. Navy Museum in Pensacola, Florida, and the other in the U.S. Marine Corps Museum in Quantico, Virginia.

Northrop X-4 Bantam While the Navy Skystreaks were still being tested, the U.S. Air Force flew its first subsonic research airplane. With swept-back wings and no horizontal tail, the little X-4 Bantam was similar to the deHavilland Swallow.

Even though the Swallow had problems, engineers knew that tailless airplanes could fly because German models had flown during World War II. The Messerschmitt Me-163 Comet was a rocket-powered interceptor plane used to attack Allied bombers. Although it did not work well because it had been rushed into service before being fully tested, it had flown.

The X-4 was designed with the help of the knowledge gained in flying the tailless Messerschmitt Me-163 Comet (above), the world's first rocket-powered fighter plane.

The Northrop X-4 was similar to the deHavilland Swallow, but it flew better.

The first X-4 flew in 1948, the second in 1949. Altogether, there were more than 100 X-4 flights before the program ended in 1954. By then, the problems that planes with swept-back wings had when they approached the sound barrier were much closer to being solved.

In 1950, the first X-4 was retired from test flying and sent to the U.S. Air Force Academy in Colorado Springs, Colorado. The second X-4 flew until 1954 and then was put on display at the U.S. Air Force Museum near Dayton, Ohio.

Bell X-5 As airplanes flew faster, they became more difficult to fly slowly for takeoff and landing. The Bell X-5 was the first airplane that could fly well at both high and low speeds. Designers realized that to fly fast, an airplane needed thin, swept-back wings. But straight wings work better at low speeds.

During World War II, the Germans had designed a wing that could be set in both straight and swept-back positions during flight. It would be set straight for takeoff and then swung back as the airplane's speed increased.

The Bell X-5 was the first successful airplane with wings whose angle could be changed during flight by moving a lever in the cockpit. Its wings are set in a forward position (above) or swept back (below).

At the end of the war, the U.S. Army captured the Messerschmitt P.1101, the German research airplane with variable-sweep wings. Still not completely built, the plane never did fly because it was later damaged in a ground accident. But the information gained from studying the Messerschmitt P.1101 made it possible to build the X-5.

The first of two X-5s flew in June 1951. A few weeks later, its wing sweep angle was changed in flight for the first time, and pilots made many tests to determine how the plane flew with its wings in different positions.

The first X-5 made many flights before it was retired to the U.S. Air Force Museum in 1955. The second X-5 crashed during a research flight to test its recovery from a spin.

Douglas X-3 Stiletto The Douglas X-3 soon joined the X-5 at the huge test center in Muroc, California. Because of its slim, streamlined shape, the Stiletto looked like the world's fastest airplane even when it was sitting on the ramp.

While engineers were building the X-3, the Westinghouse Electric Company developed a new jet engine, the J46, which was designed to put out 7,000 pounds of thrust (31 kN). Two of these engines were supposed to power the X-3.

By the time the engines were ready for flight, however, they were too big to fit into the slim airplane, and the plane's design prevented it from being made wider. The only alternative was to use smaller engines, but they would produce much less power. When the first X-3, powered by the smaller engines, flew late in 1952, there was no hope that the plane could ever reach the speed for which it had been designed to fly. If the J46 engines could

The Douglas X-3 Stiletto does not give the pilot much of a view out the windshield.

This photo of the Douglas X-3 Stiletto shows off its tiny wings and long nose.

have been used, the Stiletto might have been the first airplane to fly at *Mach 3*, three times the speed of sound. Instead, the best speed any test pilot could reach in the X-3 was just under Mach 1.

After making flights for the National Advisory Committee for Aeronautics (NACA), the first X-3's research program was completed in 1956. (NACA later became the National Aeronautics and Space Administration, or NASA.) The plane was then put on display at the U.S. Air Force Museum. A second X-3 was never completed.

23

This lopsided AD-1 scissors-wing research airplane is a pilot-carrying model, 1/10th the size of a supersonic airliner.

NASA AD-1 In the 1940s, aeronautical engineers began to design *supersonic* planes that would travel at speeds well beyond the sound barrier. The X-3, the X-4, and the X-5 were unsuccessful attempts to build supersonic airplanes, but they taught engineers about planes that flew just under the speed of sound. It was more than 25 years after the X-5 was built before engineers again became interested in subsonic research airplanes.

By 1979 when NASA flew the strange-looking AD-1 scissors-wing airplane, numerous swing-wing military airplanes were already in production for air forces around the world. The U.S. Air Force had operated large numbers of General Dynamics swing-

wing F-111 supersonic fighter-bombers for many years, and the British Tornado and the Soviet MiG-23 were also in use. Now, however, there was interest in building supersonic airliners or transports—SSTs. To fly faster than sound, these planes would have to be simpler and lighter than the military variable-sweep airplanes.

The first new idea to be tested was a one-piece wing that could be pivoted so one side could sweep forward while the other side was swept backward. The idea of a lopsided airplane did not sound very effective, but the scientists and engineers and their computers said it would work.

The first SST research airplane built was only 1/10th the size of a supersonic airliner. Then the Boeing Company, builder of many of the world's airliners, expressed an interest in building a full-size swing-wing SST. The AD-1 research airplane flew in 1980 with its wings pivoted slightly, and, the following year, it flew with its wings pivoted at a full 60-degree angle. Just as the experts had predicted, the AD-1 flew without tipping over or flying sideways.

The AD-1 is still being used for research. Although it may be many years before a scissors-wing supersonic airliner will be in operation, engineers know it can fly because of the success of the AD-1.

This collection of research airplanes includes the Douglas X-3 Stiletto (center) and (clockwise from upper right) the Bell X-5, Douglas D-558-II Skyrocket, Northrop X-4 Bantam, Bell X-1A, Douglas D-558-I Skystreak, and Convair XF-92.

Supersonic Airplanes

While some aeronautical engineers were learning how to design airplanes that could fly at just below the speed of sound, others were working on designing supersonic airplanes with powerful engines that could fly faster than sound. To accomplish this feat, engineers had to learn how to shape airplanes to make it possible for their engines to generate supersonic speed.

People had different ideas about how to design airplanes that could break through the sound barrier. Some thought an airplane with tiny, swept-back wings and a regular jet engine was needed. Others believed the barrier could be broken by a straight-winged airplane if it had enough power.

The sound barrier was considered to be a very mysterious and danger-ous zone. Yet, scientists and others had known for a long time that a properly shaped object, like a bullet, could slip through the barrier and travel much faster than the speed of sound. But because an airplane with a human being inside is much different from a bullet, research moved forward a step at a time to keep risks at a minimum.

Bell X-1 The first genuine supersonic airplane was the Bell XS-1, later called the X-1. Engineers had been thinking about this airplane since the middle of World War II, a time when most people did not even know that jet engines existed. In 1946, researchers designed and built the first X-1.

The X-1 was small, and its straight wings were thin and strong. It had a four-barrel rocket motor in its tail that produced a great amount of power and burned fuel at an amazing rate. The engine weighed only 210 pounds (95 kg) but developed 6,000 pounds of thrust (27 kN), which is equal to about 12,000 hp (9,000 kw) at top speed. With that much power, the X-1 used its entire supply of 4,680 pounds (2,106 kg) of fuel in only two and one-half minutes!

So that the X-1 would not use up most of its fuel while taking off and climbing, it was carried to high altitude under a B-29 Superfortress heavy bomber. When the B-29 reached 240 mph (384 km/h), the X-1 was released and its motor ignited. After flying under its own power for two and one-half minutes, its fuel was gone, and the motor stopped cold. Then the X-1 became a very fast glider, and the pilot would guide it back to the 12-mile (19-km)-long runway at Edwards Air Force Base, California.

After a few test flights to make certain the X-1 would fly safely, the project's scientists and engineers were ready to try to break the sound bar-rier. On October 14, 1947, Army Air Force Captain Charles E. (Chuck) Yeager was launched in the X-1 from the B-29 carrier plane.

Major Charles Yeager (left), shown here in full flying gear checking his logbook, piloted this tiny Bell X-1 that is carried into the air by a modified Boeing B-29 (above).

27

The Bell X-1 rocket-powered research plane breaks the sound barrier.

Yeager turned on the mighty little rocket motor and, in a few seconds, the X-1 was racing ahead into the unknown darkness of near sonic speed. The Mach-meter showed the plane's speed creep up past 0.9 and then the plane shuddered as it neared Mach 1. Finally, it sneaked past the speed of sound and made it to Mach 1.06. Yeager had broken through the sound barrier and was flying at 700 mph (1,120 km/h). Soon the first person to fly faster than sound glided back to earth with a huge smile on his face. A few months later, Yeager flew the X-1 at almost 1,000 mph (1,600 km/h), or Mach 1.45.

Yeager's flights had opened the door to supersonic flying, and, in a short time, the X-1's skilled pilots had shown that a carefully designed airplane could fly faster than sound without any great problems. After the historic X-1 was retired in 1950, it was sent to Washington, D.C., for display at the National Air & Space Museum.

There were other X-1s. One was wrecked in a ground accident. The X-1E flew as fast as Mach 2 and was then displayed at Edwards Air Force Base, California. In 1953, the X-1A reached a top speed of 1,650 mph (2,640 km/h). On a later flight it was destroyed while still attached to its launch airplane. The X-1B was used by NASA for a series of high-speed test flights and then exhibited in the U.S. Air Force Museum.

Chuck Yeager climbs into the cockpit of the Bell X-1 (below) and is congratulated by Laurence Bell, president of the Bell Corporation, after flying the Bell X-1A (right).

Speeding high into the atmosphere with its rocket motor blazing, the Douglas D-558-II Skyrocket research airplane flies faster than twice the speed of sound.

Douglas D-558-II Skyrocket

While the U.S. Air Force was busy breaking the sound barrier with its X-1 rocket planes, the U.S. Navy was getting ready to make history with a new version of its Skystreak. The first navy research airplane had straight wings and a jet engine. It had performed well, but the rocket-powered X-1 was faster. If the navy wanted to learn about high-speed flying, it would have to experiment with rocket power.

The navy's Skyrocket was bigger than the X-1 and had both a jet engine for flying at lower speeds and a rocket engine for supersonic flying. Its engineers soon decided, however, that they would learn more if they removed the jet engine and used the space for carrying additional rocket fuel. This would allow the Skyrocket to fly longer than the X-1.

Their idea worked. On November 20, 1953, NACA test pilot Scott Crossfield and the second Skyrocket dropped from a B-29 carrier plane. Crossfield pushed hard on the throttle, and his sleek white craft tore off into the thin air of high altitude. Before its fuel ran out, the Skyrocket reached a speed of 1,291 mph (2,066 km/h), and Crossfield became the first person to fly faster than Mach 2.

Three Douglas Skyrockets continued to fly high and fast for the navy and for NACA, sending back information that led to the design of

The Douglas D-558-II Skyrocket has just been launched from its B-29 carrier plane.

better and faster airplanes. The first Mach 2 airplane was sent to the National Air & Space Museum when the Skyrocket program ended in 1956. The others went to the Planes of Fame Museum in Chino, California, and to a museum in Lancaster, California.

Fairey FD.2 Delta Two Although the Bell and Douglas rocket airplanes could certainly fly fast, they could only fly for a few minutes. Engineers wanted an airplane that could cruise at high speeds for a longer period of time. Such a plane could help aeronautical engineers solve the new problem of the intense heat created by air friction at supersonic speed.

When air flows across the surface, or *skin*, of an airplane at high speed, the skin becomes very hot. An airliner flying at 600 mph (960 km/h) heats

The Fairey FD.2 Delta Two (WG774), at the top, was piloted by Peter Twiss to set the world air speed record in 1956. The plane was later modified with a new wing, shown in this photograph, to test the shape for the Concorde Supersonic Transport plane (SST). The other FD.2 (WG777) has the original delta wing.

up so much that, even though the outside air temperature at high altitudes may be as low as -65° Fahrenheit (-54° Celsius), the skin must be air-conditioned to keep it from melting.

In England, Fairey Aviation built a large airplane with triangle-shaped delta wings and a powerful jet engine. The engine would power the airplane to fly faster than Mach 1, but it would not use as much fuel as a rocket motor. And the sharply swept-back delta wing would help to reduce wind resistance.

A very fast airplane must be very narrow and streamlined, which makes the windshield a problem. If the windshield is too streamlined, the pilot cannot see out of it. If it is designed to give the pilot a good view, however, it will slow the airplane down.

The designers of the FD.2 solved this problem by drooping down the plane's streamlined nose and windshield during takeoff and landing so the pilot could see where the plane was going. The result was a funny-looking airplane, but the problem was solved. (The drooping nose idea worked so well it was later used on the Concorde supersonic airliner.)

The FD.2 first flew in 1954, and two years later the British were ready to try for a world air speed record. The record, set by Harold Hanes in an American F-100 jet fighter, stood at 822 mph (1,315 km/h). Flown by Peter Twiss, the Delta Two climbed to 38,000 feet (11,400 m) over the southern coast of England, the plane's power-boosting afterburner blazing away. In a few minutes, the FD.2 reached 1,132 mph (1,811 km/h) to set the new world air speed record. The record-setting FD.2 was later modified with an advanced wing shape, and it continued flying as the BAC 221. When they were retired, both FD.2s were put in museums in England.

Bell X-2 The Bell X-1 series of rocket-powered research airplanes had been such a great success that Bell began to develop the X-2 soon after the first X-1 flew. The X-2 had a fuselage much like the X-1, but it had wings and a tail that were swept back for better flying at high speed. Its motor put out 15,000 pounds of thrust (67 kN) and used even more fuel than the X-1, so fuel tanks filled every bit of extra space. Because wheels take up room when they are retracted inside an airplane, the X-2 had a nose wheel and two skids in place of the main wheels.

The first X-2 made a few test glides in 1952 and 1953, but it never flew under power. While it was being carried up to altitude for launching, it blew up, and its pilot, Skip Ziegler, was killed.

Because rocket fuel blows up easily, the threat of explosion is one of the greatest risks of high-speed flights in advanced aircraft and spacecraft. In World War II, more German rocket-powered Me-163 Comets were destroyed when they landed hard, causing

Although this Bell X-2 was destroyed before it could make its first powered flight, a second X-2 became the first airplane to fly faster than Mach 3.

the fuel to explode, than because they were shot down. More recently, on January 28, 1986, the loss of the space shuttle *Challenger* was caused by the explosion of its rocket fuel.

The second X-2 first flew in 1955 and had a more successful career. In the summer of 1956, Frank Everest became the world's fastest pilot when he flew the X-2 at 1,900 mph (3,040 km/h). That September, Ivan Kinchelow flew the X-2 to an official world altitude record of 126,000 feet (37,800 m), or almost 24 miles (38 km).

Later that month, U.S. Air Force test pilot Milburn Apt made the X-2's most historic flight. After being launched

from a B-50, Apt gave the X-2 full power and reached 2,094 mph (3,350 km/h) and Mach 3.2. No pilot had ever flown more than 2,000 mph (3,200 km/h) or Mach 3 before. But then the X-2 went out of control. Apt bailed out, but he did not survive the fall.

North American X-15 The most powerful research airplane of all was the X-15. The X-15 flew more than twice as fast and more than three times as high as any airplane before it, and its records still stand. Even though the three X-15s explored new aviation territory on almost 200 flights, only one serious accident occurred during nine years of research flying.

The X-15 was very different from any other high-speed airplane. It had tiny, short, straight wings and a large tail with wide, squared-off trailing edges instead of the usual thin, sharp trailing edges. Before each landing, the bottom part of the tail was blown off so that it would not dig into the ground.

Unlike most airplanes, the X-15 was made from stainless steel, titanium, and other new and expensive metals rather than from aluminum. Since it would be flying so fast, it was important to build the X-15 from materials that would not melt when heated to more than 1,200° Fahrenheit (650° Celsius).

The most amazing part of the new airplane was its Reaction Motors XLR-99 engine. This rocket motor weighed slightly more than 600 pounds (270 kg), or about the same as a large Cadillac V-8 engine. But when the engine ran at full power, the motor developed nearly 750,000 hp (560,000 kw) of energy and gulped rocket fuel at the rate of 10,000 pounds (4,500 kg) per minute!

The initial flight of the X-15 was made in 1959 by test pilot Scott Crossfield. Because the mighty XLR-99 motor was not yet completed, two smaller motors were used instead. Soon there were two X-15s flying and sending back data on what it was like

Test pilot Neil Armstrong is shown beside the X-15. His hand is touching the plane's "hot nose," which aids the X-15 by indicating attitude angles.

This final version of the North American X-15 carries extra fuel tanks on the bottom. It is on its way to 4,534 mph (7,297 km/h), the highest speed ever attained by an airplane.

to fly very fast after being dropped from a B-52 bomber. On the 15th flight, Joe Walker flew 2,111 mph (3,378 km/h). And Bob White climbed to 136,500 feet (40,950 m), or almost 26 miles (42 km), on the 19th flight.

When the powerful XLR-99 motors were installed in late 1960, X-15s started to show just how fast they could fly. One hit 2,830 mph (4,528 km/h) with test pilot Robert Rushworth at the controls in October 1961, and, the next month, Bob White piloted one to 4,093 mph (6,549 km/h). In only a few flights, the X-15 became the first airplane to fly faster than Mach 6.

In April 1962, Joe Walker took off from a B-52 and shot up to 246,700 feet (74,010 m)—almost 47 miles (75 km)—to nearly double the old altitude record. Several months later, Bob White zoomed to a height of 314,750 feet (94,425 m), or almost 60 miles (96 km), which is still the official world altitude record for air-launched airplanes. One year later, Walker climbed to an unofficial record of 354,200 feet (106,260 m), or 67 miles (107 km), and became the only airplane pilot to earn his wings for reaching heights usually only achieved by astronauts in spacecraft.

The highest speed ever reached by an X-15 was 4,534 mph (7,297 km/h), or Mach 6.7, a record set by Pete Knight in 1967. That speed was reached at such a high altitude that the extremely thin air could not hold back the X-15. But there was a problem flying at such heights. An airplane's control surfaces usually work against the air, like a boat's rudder works against the water. At more than 50 miles (80 km) above the earth, where the air is so thin, trying to control a plane is like trying to turn a boat with the rudder while the boat is being towed on a trailer.

To control the X-15 at high altitude, the engineers built small rockets into its nose and wingtips. When the pilot wanted to make the X-15 roll to the left, he moved the control stick left, which fired the small rocket below the right wingtip. When he wanted it to go up, he fired the small rocket on the bottom of the nose, forcing the nose up. (The space shuttle and other spacecraft use this system when they are in orbit or deep space.)

As each new speed and altitude was reached, the X-15 sent back vital information for improving research planes. Flying an X-15 was not only exciting, but it helped people learn how to build better airplanes for the future.

After 199 flights, the two surviving X-15s were finally given a rest. The first one was hung in the main hall of the National Air & Space Museum and the second was displayed in the U.S. Air Force Museum. The third X-15 broke up during reentry into the lower atmosphere after a flight to an altitude of 50 miles (80 km).

Martin X-24 After the incredible success of the X-15, a different kind of research airplane that would function as both a plane and a spacecraft was in demand. There had been a plan to launch the X-15 into orbit on the top of a huge rocket, but it was never attempted. In the late 1960s, the U.S. government wanted a special flying machine that could fly in space, survive reentry into the lower atmosphere, and then glide to a safe landing.

The Martin Company built several test aircraft to see if such a lifting-body vehicle would work. These airplanes, shaped like flattened-out versions of the early space capsules, were made from very strong metals that would not melt during reentry from space.

Even though the squashed fuselage of the lifting-body vehicle was too thick and too small to look much like an airplane's wing, this fuselage allowed the craft to fly like an airplane. If it had long, thin wings like conventional airplanes, the wings would not be able to withstand the terrific heat of reentry into the atmosphere and would quickly burn up.

The first lifting-body vehicle was the Martin X-23, a small craft that

The success of the Martin X-24A (right) and the Martin X-24B (below)—shown here on its final flight—led to the development of the space shuttle.

The Martin X-24B, dropped from a B-52 carrier plane, begins its final flight on September 23, 1975.

did not carry a pilot. It was sent up by a rocket launcher, and then it hurtled back down. Three tests in 1967 proved that the design was a good one.

Next came the X-24, a much larger version of the X-23, with a rocket motor that produced 8,000 pounds of thrust (36 kN). The X-24 was first flown in 1969. Carried up by a B-52 bomber and launched like the X-15, it reached speeds of 1,150 mph (2,150 km/h), or Mach 1.76, as it headed toward earth.

In two years, the X-24 made 28 flights and proved that an airplane with a specially-shaped fuselage and tail could be flown from high altitude to a controlled landing. Then a modified X-24 with a longer nose and a flatter bottom made another 36 flights, providing even more information on how a lifting-body vehicle works.

The X-24 was retired in 1975 and placed in the U.S. Air Force Museum. A few years later, a much larger lifting-body vehicle flew into space and then returned like an airplane. This was the space shuttle, and it owed much of its success to the tests that had been made with the Martin X-24.

The Grumman X-29 (above and below) is the first airplane with forward-swept wings to fly successfully. (Research was done on an airplane with forward-swept wings during World War II, but the plane never flew.)

When viewed from above, the X-29's odd-looking forward-swept wings are its most obvious feature.

Grumman X-29 For many years, engineers have known that it is better to sweep an airplane's wings forward than backward. Forward-swept wings do not look like they would help an airplane to move faster, but they do. A high-speed airplane with forward-swept wings will fly better and will be easier to handle at low speed, but a forward-swept wing must be stronger than a swept-back wing so it won't be twisted off by aerodynamic forces during flight.

Until recently, the only way to build a stronger forward-swept wing was to make it heavier. This, however, ruined the advantages of better design. Now lightweight, forward-swept wings can be built from new materials called *composites*. Composites combine regular metals with thin slivers of carbon or graphite, which are extremely strong and light.

The first research airplane with such a wing was the Grumman X-29. The X-29 first flew on December 14, 1984, and it has since proven so successful that the military's next generation of jet fighters will be built with forward-swept wings. Some day, civilian airplanes from executive jets to huge airliners will look like the X-29.

This composite photo shows the XC-142 tilt-wing V/STOL in four stages from takeoff through transition to forward flight. Note the changes in the position of the wing (see pages 47-48).

3

V/STOL Airplanes

While thousands of scientists and engineers were working hard to build airplanes that would fly faster, others were just as hard at work building airplanes that would fly slowly. One difficulty with modern airplanes is that they require large airports with long runways for takeoff and landing. As there is little room in the middle of cities for these airports, it often takes as long to drive to an airport as it does to fly to a distant city.

Helicopters are aircraft that are able to fly very slowly; in fact, they can *hover*, or stay motionless in midair. But helicopters cannot fly very fast, and they will probably never be able to fly much faster than they do now. The world speed record for a helicopter is 250 mph (400 km/h), while passenger airplanes regularly fly at 600 mph (960 km/h).

Today, engineers are trying to build machines that will work like both an airplane and a helicopter and can take off straight up or after only a very short roll down a runway. An airplane like this, called a *V/STOL* (*V*ertical/ *S*hort *T*ake*O*ff and *L*anding) plane, could land and take off from almost any cleared space, such as a baseball diamond or a parking lot.

Propellor-Driven V/STOLs

Some V/STOL airplanes have propellors, and others are powered by jet engines. The ones with propellors are usually quieter and use less fuel, especially while hovering. Propellor-driven V/STOL airplanes are usually part helicopter and part conventional airplane.

The Vought V-173 Flying Pancake had to sit at such a steep angle so the tips of its unusually long propellors would clear the ground.

Vought V-173 Flying Pancake

One of the first successful modern *STOL* (*S*hort *T*ake*O*ff and *L*anding) airplanes to fly was the round, flat V-173. It was built to see if such a strange shape would work well enough to be developed into a U.S. Navy fighter that would be able to take off from any field and fly faster than a navy helicopter.

This interesting idea worked surprisingly well. The V-173 first flew late in 1942 from the Vought factory in Connecticut. It had only two small 80-hp (60-kw) engines so it was not very fast, and its large, specially designed propellers worked much like the rotors on a helicopter.

The V-173 made more than 100 flights, proving that a round, flat airplane could fly very well. Engineers then proceeded with plans to build the F5U Flying Flapjack fighter, but World War II ended while the F5U was still being prepared for test flying. After the war, people were only interested in

44

jet airplanes, so the navy cancelled its program, and the F5U was broken up.

The V-173 flew for the last time in June 1947, a few days after the first well-publicized sightings of flying saucers. Some people claimed that what had been seen was actually the V-173. But while flying saucers were said to be extremely fast, the V-173 poked along at only 75 mph (120 km/h). The V-173 was later stored at the National Air & Space Museum.

Hiller X-18 In the late 1950s, several small V/STOL airplanes were flown. While none were great successes, engineers learned enough about designing such machines that they felt it was safe to construct larger ones.

One of the first full-size, propellor-driven V/STOLs was the tilt-wing Hiller X-18. Its entire wing, including engines and propellors, could be tilted so the propellors pointed straight up. When the machine was airborne, the wing could be tilted back to work like any propellor-driven airplane.

The X-18 made more than 20 preliminary flights in 1960 and 1961, but all flying tests were suddenly suspended when ground tests showed that the X-18 would run into serious problems if it tried to tilt its wings while flying. The X-18 project was not a complete failure, however, because engineers had learned so much about tilt-wing V/STOL planes that better ones could be built in the future.

With its wings and propellors pointed straight ahead, the Hiller X-18 flies like an airplane.

Curtiss-Wright X-19 The X-19 tilt-propellor V/STOL airplane had two gas turbine engines in its fuselage to drive four specially designed propellors. If one of the engines stopped running while the X-19 was flying, the other one could still drive all four propellors.

To fly vertically, the X-19 tilted its propellors so they pointed up. To fly horizontally, they were pointed forward, and the special propellors and small wings provided enough lifting force to keep the airplane in the air.

One of the two X-19s flew for the first time in 1963, and hovering tests began in 1964. Although both airplanes flew many times, the program was cancelled in 1965 because there had been so many accidents. Still,

The Curtiss-Wright X-19 V/STOL research airplane has just been rolled out of the hangar with its propellors tilted up, ready for vertical takeoff.

The LTV-Hiller-Ryan XC-142 lifts off the ground straight up like a helicopter.

engineers had learned enough about tilt-propellor V/STOL airplanes to help them on future projects.

LTV-Hiller-Ryan XC-142 Although it was used strictly for research, the XC-142 tilt-wing V/STOL airplane won a design contest for the U.S. armed forces. Five XC-142s were built and tested by the U.S. Army, Navy, and Air Force and by NASA. Their goal was to design a cargo plane and troop transport that could take off vertically and then fly at high speeds.

The tilt-wing XC-142 had four large turboprop engines mounted on a wing that could be tilted straight up or even slightly back. Then the whole wing, including the engine, could be set like a conventional airplane wing for forward flying.

The first XC-142 flew in September 1964. In a test late in December, it hovered almost motionless in midair like a helicopter. Two weeks later, the craft went up and made a full transition from vertical to horizontal motion in flight. The XC-142 had a top forward speed of 430 mph (688 km/h), and it could travel 35 mph (56 km/h) backward and carry 32 passengers or 8,000 pounds (3600 kg) of freight. In

The XC-142, with its wings and engines in the horizontal position, flies like an airplane.

five years of test flying, the XC-142 made over 400 flights. It was then put on display at the U.S. Air Force Museum.

Bell X-22 Bell Aerospace became interested in V/STOLs more than 40 years ago when they started working on their first helicopter design. Since then, Bell has built thousands of successful helicopters and has learned a great deal about machines that can fly both vertically and horizontally.

Bell began building small experimental V/STOL airplanes in the 1950s. In 1966, Bell test pilots flew the first of two X-22s powered by four tilt-duct

engines. The ducts around the propellors helped to increase the thrust of the propellors, which made it possible for the X-22 to hover much higher for longer periods of time.

The first X-22 was wrecked in a landing accident only a few months after its first flight in 1966. A second X-22 then took over the test program, making hundreds of flights. While many other experimental V/STOL airplanes could only hover close to the ground, the X-22 could hover as high as 8,000 feet (2,400 m).

Bell delivered the X-22 to the U.S. government in 1969 for testing by army, navy, and air force pilots. When

The Bell X-22 is climbing straight up (below) and converting to level flight by tilting its ducted fans forward (left).

the armed forces had finished their research, they turned the X-22 over to NASA for more tests. The X-22 continues to be operated for NASA by a private company that tests new ideas in vertical flight.

Bell XV-15 One of the most successful V/STOL test airplanes is the tilt-engine Bell XV-15, which flies well both as a helicopter and as an airplane. On each wingtip, the XV-15 has a 1,500-hp (1,120-kw) gas turbine engine that drives 25-foot (7.5-m) rotors. These rotors can be tilted up

for vertical lift-off or tilted forward for horizontal flight.

The first XV-15 flew as a helicopter in 1977, and the second one made the first in-flight conversion from helicopter to airplane in 1979. The difficult test program went slowly, but, in 1983, one of the XV-15s was flying so well it was shown to the aviation world at the Paris Air Show. The XV-15 made a big hit as it took off like a helicopter and then flew level at high speed like a modern airplane.

The XV-15 test airplanes can carry as many as nine passengers and can

With its rotor blades facing forward, the Bell XV-15 flies forward like an airplane.

This version of the V-22 Osprey—the Bell-Boeing MV-22A—was designed for the U.S. Marines.

fly as fast as 350 mph (560 km/h), which is much faster than the fastest helicopter. They can land and take off from any cleared space big enough to park on. The future of this kind of tilt-engine V/STOL looks good, and Bell Aerospace has plans to build a larger version of the XV-15 that can carry 20 passengers.

The newest tilt-engine V/STOL is the V-22 Osprey. The V-22 is being developed by Bell Aerospace and the Boeing Company for the U.S. Marine Corps which intends to use it for transporting troops into battle like helicopters have done for many years. The V-22, however, will be much faster than a helicopter, which will enable it to bring more troops to the field with less chance of being shot down by the enemy.

The Short SC.1 takes off from a ramp designed for V/STOL takeoff and landing (below) and becomes airborne (above).

Jet-Propelled V/STOLs

At the same time that many engineers were developing propellor-driven V/STOL aircraft, others were busy trying to build jet-propelled V/STOLs. Ideally, jet-propelled V/STOLs should be able to fly faster than those with propellors, and some might even be able to fly faster than the speed of sound. These airplanes are especially useful for supporting ground troops in battle, as they can operate from a clearing in a jungle or from a beach. Since they do not need a long runway or an aircraft carrier for taking off, they can stay close to the action. They can take off, attack the enemy, and get back to their base in a few minutes to reload for another attack. These aircraft may be the military V/STOLs of the future.

Short SC.1 One of the first successful jet V/STOLs was an odd-looking little delta-winged plane from Northern Ireland. The SC.1 had a conventional jet engine to drive it forward. Four additional jet engines, which took air in from the top of the fuselage and shot a hot blast out the bottom, were mounted vertically in the middle of the fuselage.

The SC.1's four vertical engines were used only for takeoff and landing. Once the craft was in the air, the vertical engines were shut off, and the jet engine propelled the plane forward.

The SC.1 could take off from any space as large as itself, and it could land in a space as small by turning its four engines back on.

The first SC.1 flew in 1957, and it made its first vertical takeoff the following year. In 1960, it took off straight up and then changed to forward flight, making its first midair transition. It took three years for engineers to perfect this new way of flying. Test pilots, accustomed to airplanes that took off straight ahead on long runways, also had to learn a lot of new maneuvers.

Flying the SC.1 led directly to the most successful of all the V/STOL airplanes, the Harrier. One of the remaining SC.1s was put on display in a transportation museum in Northern Ireland and the other was stored at the Science Museum in London, England.

Hawker P.1127 The most famous V/STOL airplane built over the past 30 years was the Harrier. Built by the British Aerospace Aircraft Group for the air forces of many countries, including the United States, the Harrier started out in 1960 as the Hawker P.1127 research airplane. Unlike other jet-propelled V/STOLs, the P.1127 used only one engine for both vertical and level flying, so it did not have to drag along lift engines when it was flying straight. Instead, the exhaust pipes of its huge jet engine were tilted downward to fly vertically. That way,

This Hawker P.1127, forerunner of the British Aerospace Harrier V/STOL fighter, made its first vertical takeoff in October 1960.

it could carry a heavier load than V/STOLs with two or more engines.

The P.1127's first flight was *tethered*, which means the plane was held down by strong cables to prevent it from rising very high or tipping over. A month after its first flight, the P.1127 hovered without cables. In 1961, it flew like a conventional airplane, and, before the year was over, it had made a full transition from vertical takeoff to level flight in the air.

In 1965, six improved P.1127s were built as Hawker Kestrel fighters. These Kestrels were used in a special test squadron to see if a V/STOL airplane could be used for combat. Military test pilots from Great Britain, West Germany, and the United States took

part in this squadron and flew hundreds of training missions. They staged mock air battles between the Kestrels and conventional jet fighters, and the Kestrels usually won.

Britain's Royal Air Force soon ordered a new version of the Kestrel, called the Harrier, and the U.S. Marine Corps bought a large number of them. A special version, the Sea Harrier, was built to fly from an aircraft carrier and prompted the development of a new kind of aircraft carrier deck, one with an upward curving slope. Because they did not need to use all of their engine power to get into the air, Harriers could take off from this "ski jump" deck with a heavier load of fuel and weapons.

Right: These four
Hawker Siddeley
Kestrels were
tested by a joint
U.S./British/West
German unit and
were found to be
successful in com-
bat. Below: A
Hawker Siddeley
Harrier is prepared
for a flight.

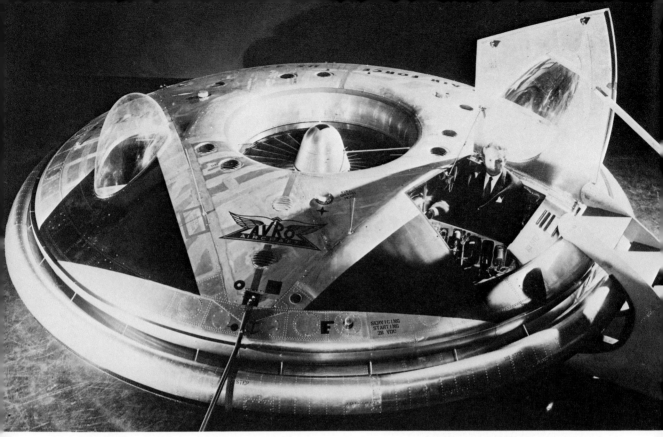

The man is seated in one of the two cockpits of the unsuccessful Avro VZ-9V Avrocar "flying saucer." Air for its three jet engines is taken in through the hole in the center.

The first Hawker P.1127 was put on display in the Royal Air Force Museum near London, England, and there are Kestrels at the National Air & Space Museum and at the U.S. Air Force Museum.

Avro VZ-9V Avrocar If it had flown, the Avrocar would have been a true "flying saucer." Round and flat without any wings or tail, the two-person Avrocar had three small jet engines that were supposed to make the craft rise straight up and then fly at 300 mph (480 km/h) at high altitude. The engines shot a blast out the bottom of the outer ring, which made the Avrocar take off on a cushion of air. To fly forward, the blast was sent out of the rear of the aircraft.

Two Avrocars were built in Canada in the late 1950s for the U.S. government. They were tested and modified and then tested again, but neither was able to rise more than a few inches off the ground. When the Avrocar flew forward—even at low speed—it wobbled badly.

Engineers thought the Avrocar might work with larger engines and the addition of an automatic stabilizer system, but nearly $20,000,000 had already been spent on the project. The government did not want to spend more, so the project was cancelled in 1961. One of the two discs was displayed at the U.S. Army's Transportation Corps Museum in Fort Eustis, Virginia, and the other was stored at the National Air & Space Museum.

Dornier Do.31 The West German Do.31 V/STOL research airplane looked like a small cargo plane with a pod added to each wingtip. Each pod contained four small jet engines used for takeoff and landing. Doors at the top of the pods opened to take air in and a jet blast was sent out the bottom, which pushed the airplane up or let it down gently. During level flight, these engines stood idle.

The first Do.31 flew early in 1961. A few months later, the second Do.31 took off straight up and then made a transition to level flight. In 1969, an experimental Do.31 flew from its test base in West Germany to the Paris Air Show, a distance of 423 miles (677 km), which set a world record for jet-lift aircraft.

The Do.31 made a terrific amount of noise and was unable to lift much more than its test equipment. When

The Dornier Do.31 is being shown at the Hanover (West Germany) Air Show in 1970.

The Dornier Do.31 uses engines mounted on its wingtips for lifting off the ground and has separate jet engines for forward flight.

the Do.31's first test flights were completed, it was displayed in the Deutsches Museum in Munich, West Germany.

Boeing/NASA QSRA The *QSRA* (*Quiet, Short-haul Research Airplane*), a fairly conventional four-engine jet cargo plane, has engines mounted on top of its wings. The jet blasts air back over the wing to create additional lift. The air blows over the wing flaps to make them work even when the airplane is flying at a steep upward angle.

When the QSRA is ready to take off, the pilot lowers the flaps and gives the airplane full power. The incoming air and the air from the jet blasts pouring over the wings create an enormous amount of lift. After a short roll down the runway, the QSRA leaves the ground and climbs steeply into the sky.

One of the most important features of the QSRA is its lack of noise. It has special insulation inside its engine covers. By climbing and descending steeply, it reduces its landing and takeoff time, which further reduces its noise level.

The QSRA is still being tested by NASA at Langley Field in Virginia. When its test flights are finished, it will probably be sent to a museum where people can see this important V/STOL research airplane.

Because of insulation inside the engine covers and an ability to take off from a short runway and climb steeply, the Boeing/NASA QSRA creates measurably less noise than a conventional airplane.

Piloted by Jeana Yeager and Dick Rutan (left), the *Voyager* (above) was neither a high-speed nor a V/STOL research airplane. Instead, it was designed to find out if an airplane could circle the earth without stopping to refuel. It did, landing on December 23, 1986, after a nine-day flight.

4

The Future of
Research Airplanes

Because they offer opportunities to learn so much about designing and building better airplanes, new research airplanes will continue to be built for many years to come. Some will be scaled-down ½-size or ¾-size airplanes that can be built and tested less expensively than full-size airplanes. And no doubt others will be super-secret military research airplanes that fly from test bases in the Mojave Desert north of Los Angeles, California, from the wilderness north of Las Vegas, Nevada, or from Ramenskoye, a base southeast of Moscow in the U.S.S.R. All of these areas are off-limits to the public, far from homes and roads, so these planes will be seen by the public only when their testing is over and they are put on display. Then these planes can be added to the list of aircraft that have helped aeronautical science to move forward.

Just as the Wright brothers built special airplanes to test their new ideas, research airplanes today continue to test design and engineering ideas that someday may be seen in conventional airplanes.

INDEX

In 1956, Peter Twiss flew this Fairey Delta II at 1,132 mph (1,811 km/h) to set a new world air speed record (see pages 31-33).

ACKNOWLEDGMENTS: The photographs in this book are reproduced through the courtesy of: pp. 1, 18, 31, McDonnell Douglas Corporation; pp. 2, 49, 50, Bell Aerospace; pp. 6, 8 (bottom), 9, 10, 14, 40, 41, Grumman Corporation; p. 8 (top), Lockheed-California Company; p. 11, 21 (top), 22, 25, 27 (bottom), 28, 45, 46, 56, U.S. Air Force; p. 13, Library of Congress; pp. 17, 54, 55 (top), British Aerospace Corporation; pp. 19, 27 (top), 29, 30, 44, Smithsonian Institution; pp. 20, 21 (bottom), 23, 24, 34, 35, 36, 38, 39, 48, 59, 63, National Aeronautics and Space Administration; p. 32, Fairey Aviation, Ltd.; pp. 42, 47, LTV Corporation; p. 51, Bell-Boeing; p. 52, Short Brothers, Ltd.; pp. 55 (bottom), 57, 58, Don Berliner; p. 60 (top), Voyager Aircraft; p. 60 (bottom), National Aeronautical Association; p. 64, Flight International. Cover photographs courtesy of Grumman Corporation (front) and Bell Aerospace (back).